B[illegible]OL BLITZ

The Untold Story

Helen Reid

REDCLIFFE
Bristol

First published in 1988 by
Redcliffe Press Ltd, 49 Park Street, Bristol 1

ISBN 0 948265 82 5

*Typeset and printed in Great Britain by
Penwell Ltd, Parkwood, Callington, Cornwall*

Contents

COLMANS
STARCH
NESTLE
SWISS
MILK
CITY GROUND
CARDIFF CITY
PAULTON
SOUTHAMPTON

Introduction

It took the 1982 Falklands conflict to remind us how our news is managed and censored during a war.

This was even more true of World War Two, when official censorship was such that for example, Bristol newspapers had to inform their blitzed readers of the bombing of a 'West town', and were only allowed to reveal that it was in fact Bristol some days after the raid had happened.

To keep up morale and avoid giving any information or comfort to the enemy, the local press published the briefest of information about the damage and loss of life; they printed only upbeat and humorous stories of courage and determination.

They were forced to leave out reports of the grumbles and arguments, the shortages and inefficiencies, criticism of local administration, and battles over shelters: this would have been pandering to 'defeatism'.

Accordingly, many stories of the Bristol Blitz went untold. This book is an attempt to reveal some of them.

While there were many acts of courage, and a popular feeling that 'Bristol Could Take It', there were also panic, depression, disorganisation and open rebellion, all of which went unreported at the time.

Now that the Bristol Blitz is almost fifty years in the past, this other history ought to be told for the sake of a balanced record.

The information comes partly from now-released official documents and partly from the verbatim memories of some of the people involved. The photographs, many of which were not published, because they were not passed by the Ministry of Information censors, were taken by Bristol press photographers working for the *Western Daily Press,* the *Evening World* and the *Evening Post.*

My thanks go to the Bristol Record Office, the Trustees of the Mass Observation Unit, Sussex University, the Public Record Office at Kew, Bristol United Press, to the many Bristolians who responded to my requests for information, and to Robin Marleyn for help with research, and advice. Thanks also go to Martin Chainey for the preparation of the photographs.

Note on the photographs: 'Passed' and 'not passed' indicate whether the censor passed the picture for publication or not; the captions in quotation marks are the ones approved or not approved by the wartime censors.

Opposite: The Victorian corner shop had already swallowed up one of the five gables of the Llandoger Trow in King Street, and a bomb in 1940 reduced the gables to the present three.

The Dutch House after the November 24th raid, which as the clock shows, happened at 10.20pm. Could this much-loved landmark have been saved?

1 — 'Nazi frightfulness came west last night'

The one thing that everyone is hungry for during a war is information.

And that was just what the Ministry of Information, a truly Orwellian title, wanted to suppress. The Ministry was concerned with controlling and managing information rather than with spreading it.

Disgruntled Bristolians would see their city shattered by a raid, and then read a headline like the one at the beginning of the chapter; in this case the *Evening World*, who gave no details of where the raid took place, what was bombed, how many died, or which factories, businesses and streets were hit.

They were simply not allowed to. The Ministry of Information issued a set statement which the papers and radio could publish, and then a few days later, when the Air Ministry was satisfied that the Germans had indeed intended to bomb Bristol, the fact that the West town in question was Bristol was released.

Every newspaper editor was given documents known as the Defence Notices, listing subjects on which nothing could be published. They received a stream of notices and memos (one editor said he had 5,000 of them) adding to the list of banned topics. Weather forecasts were banned, for example; no mention of power stations or factories was allowed; and the MOI even suggested the editorial handling of certain topics. In theory, comment was free, and the national press was indeed critical of the management of the war, but provincial editors played the game, and consulted the MOI on anything they thought might be controversial.

Censorship was so strict that even births, marriages and deaths columns were vetted to see if there was any mention of the locations or movements of servicemen or ships. (No names of ships were ever mentioned: the censors even struck out references to HMS Pinafore!)

No readers' letters that might be critical of local authorities or the government were ever published, and even advertisements which indicated that a shop had moved premises because of the bombing were ruled out; Moss Bros in Bristol got into trouble in December 1940 for an advertisement which gave an indication of the extent of their damage, and their location.

With the best of motives, the public was left in the dark. After a heavy raid, Bristolians would naturally be anxious about relatives in another part of the city—but the papers could give no details of which streets had been bombed. Information was posted only in the streets.

Photographs were equally censored: all that were taken had to be submitted to the censor, who stamped them either 'Passed for publication' or 'Not to be published.'

Photographs of demolished factories, shops, historic buildings, churches, or hospitals were not published, not only because they could show the enemy that their bombing had been effective, but because they might lower morale of the citizens who lived in the area. No pictures of raging fires, rescues, or of bodies, were used, nor photos showing people who were distressed and frightened.

Only morale-boosting pictures, of victims carrying on regardless despite the rubble, of cheerful people salvaging furniture from their homes, of cheery notices outside bomb-blasted shops—'no window cleaners required'—were allowed. Queues were not photographed, nor were shelters, crying children, or homeless animals. No pictures of the trekkers who left the city nightly were ever seen.

Since the citizens of Bristol knew the reality of the Blitz, this censorship caused great resentment. They felt they were not trusted, and that the civil authorities were trying to pull the wool over their eyes, as well as the enemy's.

Since it was impossible to complain via the newspapers without being labelled a Communist or a subversive, people took to writing letters of protest to their local councillors, to the Lord Mayor, to their MPs, to members of the Cabinet and to the Royal family. Deprived of hard information, people relied on rumours. The first of hundreds of rumours came in 1939, with a false tale of shortages of tea and coffee that resulted in huge queues outside Carwardines.

Rumours in Bristol during the Blitz ranged from the hopeful to the ridiculous: it was said that some of the bombs dropped were filled only with sawdust, that the Germans bombed Arno's Vale cemetery because they thought the gravestones were lines of army tents, and that contaminated food was being sold from warehouses that were bombed and open to weather.

After the Baedeker raid on Bath, it was believed that bodies were laid out in the fields nearby because the mortuaries were full. The 'bodies' were in fact sleeping people who had taken to the countryside for safety. It was also believed in Bristol that the citizens of Bath were starving, and that they would all be evacuated.

Another persistent rumour was that a new and virulent strain of flu, caused by the raids, had arrived in the city. The Emergency Committee blamed milk and bread roundsmen for spreading the bad news.

Rumour spreading was such a regular sport in Bristol that the local MOI tried to run an Anti-Rumour Campaign, getting people to take a pledge not to spread gossip, and to report all rumour-mongers to the police. An advertisement in the local press proclaimed Rumour-Mongers Are Bad Citizens, but the grapevine went on regardless.

Some of the rumours did have a basis in fact: the stories of petrol and coal shortages in the winter of 1941 were indeed true. Sir Hugh Elles had to demand immediate action from the Minister for Home Security, Herbert Morrison, when coal stocks were down to one week's supply. He wrote in a secret report of an 'impending calamity': 'Nothing short of another air attack would depress public morale as much as empty grates.'

It was simply the lack of information that drove people wild: it led them, in Bristol particularly, as Mass Observers noted, to listen regularly to the Lord Haw-Haw pro-German propaganda broadcasts. 'They gave the same information as the BBC, but two days sooner', was the justification one observer overheard.

Another odd by-product of censorship was the development of a kind of league table of suffering in provincial cities. Days before the terrible raid of November 24th, when the shopping centre and Park Street were hit, films of the destruction of Coventry had been shown in Bristol cinemas. But Bristol's big raid received no similar publicity, and this caused jealousy. (In fact, in terms of total blitz casualties, Bristol came sixth in the 'league' with 1,159 deaths, fewer than Liverpool and Merseyside, Birmingham, Clydeside and Coventry).

'We've been told that it's been worse down here than it was in Coventry or Birmingham, but we haven't had as much said about us. Anyone'd think that Coventry people were the only ones who could take it,' was a typical protest.

Another complained that Bath, a few miles away, had not suffered at all—though of course Bath's turn was to come.

So casualty figures were grossly exaggerated and there were wild stories about the local ack-ack defence posts running out of ammunition. It was the rumour that the defence of Bristol was not being managed properly that led to Churchill being booed when he came to visit Bristol on April 12th, 1941. The censors promptly put out a statement saying that the booing never happened!

Many bungles and muddles also went unreported.

The Regional Commissioner Sir Hugh Elles, giving an official account of the November 24th raid, decided to omit from his final version the fact that decoy fires to trick the German bombers were not lit because the expert supposed to light them could not be found.

Part-time auxiliary fireman Cliff Lachem remembers the confusion and inefficiency of the night when his team from Radstock was called in to help fight the November 24th fire storm.

'We entered Victoria Street and this was like Dante's Inferno, raging fires in the buildings, belching out of the windows and doors, and the wind was like a tornado. The flames were hundreds of feet high, the heat was terrific, even the shop window glass was melting.

'I should think we were the last to go up Victoria Street that night. We got through all right and then on to Bristol Bridge, and then left into Baldwin Street; looking back we could see the Castle Street area was all afire, and so on into the Centre and round into Bridewell HQ.

'We reported our arrival, collected our orders: we were to go back to the Temple Meads approach, which we had passed on the way in. We had to uncouple in order to turn round, and find a back way round . . . This raid found a lot of faults in the organisation, and one of the worst was the fact of having to go to the centre of Bristol to report. This was altered by the next raid, when you had to report to Fire Officers on the outskirts of the city.'

Nor did it emerge until years later how inadequate the fire-fighting facilities had been in a city that had two rivers and the docks to call on for water. On November 24th, 70 fires were reported, and some needed five to ten pumping appliances each. But there were only 224 available—the rest had broken down, or were incomplete. The regular Fire Brigade was understrength by 77 men, and only 995 firemen were in service, enough to man 96 appliances. The rest were manned by 897 part-time firemen.

Private towing vehicles had to be borrowed to pull the trailer pumps, and since it was a Sunday, there was no public transport for the part-timers to get into the centre of the city. Some fire appliances could not be used because they ran out of petrol, and there were no petrol stations open to provide more, again because it was Sunday.

Damage to trunk water mains inevitably caused a shortage of water, and 77 outside brigades were asked for help, but mostly they arrived too late. Bad supervision and lack of experience, shortage of men and working appliances meant that the heart of the city burned far more fiercely than it need have done. Firemen found they also had to do rescue work wherever the rescue services were unable to get through.

In fact, post-mortems on the November 24th raid suggest, with hindsight, that more buildings were lost than need have been: a report said that a great many of the ancient city churches could have been saved if their congregations had organised fire-watching; the Dutch House was pulled down by the army two days after the raid, despite an assessment that only the top floors were badly damaged on one side, and that the much-loved landmark could have been restored. Nobody had the time to organise a protest and insist on its conservation.

A very serious blunder that may have cost lives happened during the raid on March 16th, 1941. In the middle of the raid, the All Clear was sounded, and people began to leave their shelters and make for home or to come out of their basements and go upstairs. But the bombs continued to rain down, and minutes later, the alert was sounded again.

There was no official explanation, of course, so rumours started that ammunition at the ack-ack batteries had run out, that a cease-fire had been ordered, that the anti-aircraft fire was stopped to allow a local fighter squadron to take off, but it had failed to do so. This bungle sapped public confidence and morale and led to rumours of exaggerated casualty figures. Bristolians genuinely believed that 800-1,000 died in this raid: in fact, the death toll—grim enough—was 257.

The scepticism about Bristol's defence was well-founded; after all, when the September 25th daylight raid on Bristol Aeroplane works at Filton was reported on the BBC, the bulletin said that no enemy raiders had penetrated our defences! In fact, no fighters were put up against the German bombers until September 27th, when a squadron was hastily based at Filton.

Bristol, shaken and angry at the ease with which Luftwaffe pilots were able to fly in immaculate formation over the Dorset coast and make straight for Bristol, claimed there was a gap in the ack-ack defences. So in September 1940, Alderman Frank Parrish, chairman of the Emergency Committee, paid a top secret visit to Ernest Bevin, Minister of Labour, to complain, and within a week the gap in the city's ground defences had been filled with 4 of the most modern anti-aircraft guns available.

But the warning system still sometimes failed: on June 27th, 1941, enemy aircraft were actually seen overhead and anti-aircraft guns went into action, but no air raid warning was sounded.

Another tragic blunder happened in the case of the daylight Broad Weir bombing of August 28th, 1942, when three busloads of people were killed.

The siren went some minutes *after* the incident, and the firefighting and rescue services were delayed in getting there by inefficient handling of the traffic. Moreover, the buses did not receive a direct hit but caught fire from the flying fragments and burning petrol from a car that was bombed. They burned out before the fire engines could get through to them. No fault was found with the emergency exits in the buses.

Other bungles were organisational: early in the war there was an order to arrange for the reception of thousands of refugees from Belgium and Holland. They never arrived, because Bristol was not a designated reception area for refugees, but nevertheless preparations were made.

Then in June 1940, the Medical Officer of Health in Bristol asked for 700-800 beds in Bristol hospitals to be vacated for military casualties who never arrived. This understandably caused great dissatisfaction among the displaced patients and their relatives.

Another reason for these annoying mix-ups was the fault of the system: the organisation of voluntary and official services was a tangled web of responsibilities. Local authority responsibilities overlapped with Civil Defence duties, and often charities and voluntary organisations had to step in and do their jobs. The Citizens' Advice Bureau, for example, found itself dealing with the problems of the homeless, and with charges of profiteering, things it was never intended to cope with.

Lack of official information caused confusion: meat shortages happened because, according to the aptly-named Tom Lamb, Bristol's Food Officer, some butchers were refusing to take their full supplies because they anticipated that the demand would be smaller. The butchers argued that so many bombed homes had been left without cooking facilities that Bristol housewives would not buy meat! They also refused to store meat in their refrigerators on the grounds that gas supplies might fail, and the meat would rot.

Another topic never publicly discussed was Bristol's attitude to 'conchies'. Conscientious objectors were put to work at the Portishead Generating Station and the Corporation's Albert Road depot, and there the majority of other workers got up a petition asking that the conchies be segregated and forbidden to do any war-work, despite the shortage of manpower. A team of doctors and students at Bristol University begged to be allowed to give medical aid by joining the casualty service during raids, but were refused permission because they were conchies.

Equally unreported were the many dismissals of Civil Defence workers for slacking, sleeping at their posts, drunkeness and crime.

There was also a tendency to dismiss every comment and criticism as the agitation of communists: on the Filwood Park estate in June 1940, there was disorder when police investigated the issuing of subversive pamphlets; the editor of the Bristol Co-op publication *The Citizen* had his house entered by five plainclothes policemen who kept his wife and daughter in one room and him in another while they searched the house for subversive material.

They found nothing, and it emerged that information had been given which, in the eyes of the authorities, necessitated an immediate search: he was suspected of being a fifth columnist.

Another event which caused extreme distrust was a march by women of Knowle West during the coal shortage of early 1941. They held banners saying 'Knowle West Women Will Not Die Shivering' and 'Butter Not Guns'. This too was thought to be communist-inspired, as were the widespread complaints about shelters.

There was more mismanagement over evacuation. Part of Bristol had been designated at the beginning of the war as a 'neutral' area, which meant in fact that evacuees could be sent *to* Bristol, rather than away from it. Some homeless Londoners were evacuated to a seven-mile belt round the city, and many soldiers were also billeted in the area; thus when the blitz on Bristol began, there were not enough official places nearby for Bristol children. So unofficial evacuation began, with parents paying for private billets, and thereby bidding up the price.

A visit from the Minister of Health was needed to convince the authorities that 5-14 year-olds should be evacuated—by which time there were few billets left. It took until February 1941 for 12,000 children a week to be evacuated out of Bedminster, Avonmouth, Shirehampton, Hotwells, Barton Hill, St. Pauls and Mina Road, and most had to go to Cornwall or Devon.

Evacuation was also hampered by persistent rumours that those who went to certain areas, such as West Town and Backwell, were being ill-treated.

Other facts of war life went unmarked: it was not reported until much later that seventy-eight people fell into the Floating Harbour because of the blackout; fortunately no-one drowned, though one woman died from falling into a static water tank.

There was no word of the running battles that police fought with motorists whose headlights were insufficiently camouflaged; there was a strange theory that since Bristol was built on hills, when a car went uphill, its headlights shone into the sky and gave away the position of the city to enemy aircraft!

Sometimes whole crowds joined in the punch-ups over car lights, as on March 17th, 1941, when a crowd mobbed a car with an unmasked headlight and a fight ensued. Saturday night brawls in the Centre were common, and later in the war, there were a few confrontations of British and American soldiers, including a notable fight in Park Street.

Though the newspapers did not say so, the opinion of the average Bristolian about the management of the war, was that local government was slow and conservative, and far too ready to listen to the advice of the wealthier inhabitants, according to Mass Observation reports. 'You can trust Bristol' said one housewife. 'If anyone is going to be slack and make a mess of things, it will be Bristol.'

Not passed. Wholesale destruction of Stafford Street Bedminster, where residents are trying to salvage some of their belongings.

Passed but only after the censor had scratched out the names on the shop signs in Park Street.

BIG NIGHT RAID ON WEST TOWN

Churches, Schools, and Homes Hit

A West town had its heaviest air raid of the war last night. Flares were followed by incendaiary and high explosive bombs, as the raiders appeared to pass over in waves at intervals of a few minutes. Very intense anti-aircraft fire opened up, and the barrage was maintained throughout the raid. It was reported that churches, schools, and a large number of private houses were among the places set on fire.

; The men of the fire and A.R.P. services performed stupendous labours in bringing the fires under control.

A number of casualties were feared.

Indiscriminate bombing resulted in damage in several parts of the town last night.

Although no particulars were available early this morning it was stated that the casualties were comparatively few.

Among the buildings hit were a school and a church in the crypt of which a large number of people had sought shelter, and all of them escaped.

Amazing stories were told of narrow escapes.

Shot Down after Attack in West

After it had been machine-gunned a West of England aerodrome a Dornier 215 bomber was shot down in the English Channel yesterday afternoon by Spitfires of the Fighter Command, states the Air

Circumstances have compelled the holdiug over of certain features and advertisements. They will appear to-morrow.

GREEKS ENTER POGRADETZ

Italians Flee in Disorder

Greek advanced units entered Pogradetz yesterday afternoon. They have passed through the town and are on the main road leading to Elbasan.

The small mountain town of Moscopolis, 10 miles west-north-west of Koritza, also fell to Greek troops yesterday.

One entire Italian division has been broken up in disorder, while reports from Koritza state that three further battalions have been scattered and are being chased

All that the *Evening Post* could print about the November 24th/25th raid.

Not passed. Children were not encouraged to handle unexploded incendiary bombs, as this trio did in their garden at Almondsbury.

Not passed for obvious reasons. These three photographs must be the most horrific taken in the entire Bristol Blitz. They show the carnage in Broad Weir, minutes after the early morning bomb which destroyed three busloads of people on August 24th, 1942.

Not passed, because it showed damage to a commercial building, in this case E.S. & A. Robinson in Victoria Street.

Not passed. 'Stairs of a Bristol public building where Royalty and many famous people have trod, is now littered with wreckage after a fire caused by Nazi night raiders.' It was in fact the Merchants Hall, Marsh Street.

Passed. 'This statue of the Virgin Mary escaped damage during an air raid which caused considerable havoc to a convent in a South-West town. No-one was injured.' The Convent of the Good Shepherd was at Arno's Court, Brislington.

Not passed. The pathetic and surreal results of a bomb on the Bristol Museum, Queen's Road.

Left: Not passed. Photos of blitzed churches were rarely published because of the risk of lowering morale. This was the scene at St. Clement's Church, Newfoundland Road.

Below: Not passed, as it shows an injured person being rescued by the Bomb Squad.

Not passed. 'Not bowed down. The spirit of Bristol, courageously and grimly withstanding the onslaught of enemy bombs, is well symbolised in this picture of the City's coat of arms perched high on the ruined walls of a public building.' But where?

Not passed. Metal Agencies Co. building at the back of Queen Square.

Not passed, because these 'innocent cottagers surveying their few salvaged possessions' did not look happy. The cottage was at Stoke Gifford.

2 — *'Morale in Bristol has been left to drift'*

Mass Observation report, December 1940

It is probably just as well that Bristol never learned about a secret report on its morale during the Blitz.

For while Bristolians thought they were coping with the Blitz as well as any other city, the secret report said that Bristolians were more depressed, more nervy, and more defeatist than the people of Coventry, Plymouth and Southampton.

Morale, and the fostering of it, was the keynote of the propaganda war on the home front in World War Two. But how do you measure it?

Mass Observation, started in 1937 as a grass roots social survey organisation, had its fingers on the pulse of the nation. It selected volunteers to keep diaries, and go around listening for comments on selected topics: they would eavesdrop on conversations in pubs and shops and cinemas, and record reactions.

Several Mass Observers, who must still remain anonymous, were keeping their eyes and ears open in Bristol during the Blitz.

But Mass Observation also had a special investigation team which went round blitzed cities, after the raids, to assess morale and public attitudes, and their report on Bristol caused a secret furore.

For the team, which visited Bristol three times at intervals between December 19th, 1940 and April 2nd, 1941, came to the conclusion that Bristol was suffering from poor morale and unimaginitive leadership.

It was this latter charge which caused the secret outrage, for the independent MO report was never intended for publication, and so did not mince words. It was prepared regardless of official accounts, departmental feelings, or patriotic propaganda.

The few civic leaders and Cabinet Ministers who did see it complained to Herbert Morrison, who, after reading it, demanded the withdrawal of all copies. The local dignitaries complained that it was the work of 'a few intellectuals with nothing better to do.'

High-ranking officials described it an an extraordinary mixture of fact, fiction and dangerous mischief, and Morrison resented the circulation of what he felt was 'ill-founded criticism without any attempt to check accuracy.'

So the document remained secret, and did not become available until the mid-seventies.

The report said that Bristolians were coping far less well with the raids than people in other parts of the country. The population was less cheerful: they did not joke about the raids, they gathered morbidly for weeks around the bomb-sites, they listened regularly to the broadcasts by Lord Haw-Haw, indulged in defeatist talk, and spread rumours.

'We found nothing like the dislocation and multiple personal discomforts which still dominate private and domestic life in Southampton or Coventry,' said the investigators, who found a fortnight after the November 24th raid that telephones were working, hot food was being supplied to the homeless, and that bomb damage was less than in Coventry or Southampton. 'Despite all this, there is more depression in Bristol than in any other area studied in recent months.'

'There is a quite open defeatism, especially among the young workers, though the Lord Mayor and others appear to have a somewhat exaggerated idea of its potentialities. There is also much more wishful thinking about the war soon being over than in other areas, in itself probably an indication of depression.

'There is less laughter and cheerfulness in Bristol than in Southampton or other places at an equivalent period after main raids. Haw-Haw rumours are exceptionally abundant. This again is an oblique indication of lowered morale. The investigators found more Haw-Haw listening than ever before. Other rumours are also common.

'The main grumble is about the shelters. There is a violent minority dissatisfaction with Bristol shelters and this is certainly often spontaneous, non-political, and actually justified.

'Investigators with a wide comparison of experience with town shelter facilties consider those in Bristol to be strikingly inferior and inadequate in many parts of the town.'

The local Mass Observers collected some damning quotes from Bristolians, showing their defeatism: 'I can't see how we're going to win this war.' 'Why don't we call an armistice?' 'Of course we're losing, we're only one little country.' They reported that 12 days after the November 24th raid, people were still gazing at the wrecked buildings and saying gloomily: 'It'll never be the same again'.

They noted a particular Bristol phenomenon, the widespread reliance on the national newspapers' astrologers, especially the optimistic ones like Lyndoe who said the stars showed the war would be over in a year.

On their second visit to Bristol, in March 1941, the MO blitz investigators found Bristolians still grumbling about the lack of credit and limelight they had been given for their sufferings. They were also blaming Lord Beaverbrook for Bristol's heavy raids, because in the *Daily Express* he had compared Bristol in size and status to a similar German town bombed by the RAF. They believed that the Luftwaffe was now taking reprisals because of this.

The investigators noted that Bristolians felt they alone in Britain were suffering, and that no-one cared, and added that the visit of King George VI in December, 1940 had been of value 'because it makes a town feel that their suffering is linked, through the king, to the whole nation. There is always a tendency for a blitzed town to feel that its disaster is a purely local and largely personal affair.'

They concluded: 'We should say that morale in Bristol is being left to drift in its own direction far too much, and that there is a dangerous lack of imaginitive leadership and especially a rather poor quality of local leadership in this area. It would seem quite possible that depression and defeatist feelings which at present only exist in embryo might heavily and quite rapidly increase in Bristol unless something is done to give the people positive feelings of pride and purpose.'

The immediate reaction of the Corporation to the devastating MO reports was to commission its own survey of Bristol morale, and since the results of a survey depend on the questions you ask, this one produced just the answer the city fathers wanted. It concluded that Bristol morale was magnificent.

Bristol's own survey on morale was carried out during three weeks in April 1941, with questionnaires going to voluntary bodies, representatives of the professions, businesses, trade unions and housewives. A thousand answers were received, and from these, the conclusions were that permanent morale had not declined in any appreciable way.

The survey did find that Bristolians were tired (a 'Sleep More' campaign was launched!) that children were too exhausted by night raids to go to school, and that spiritual life in the city needed reviving. People complained of the lack of deep shelters, slow repairs to damaged homes, poor public transport, and lack of small luxuries.

The local report came to this splendidly Churchillian conclusion: 'Their spirit is high. It is the duty of their leaders to see that it remains high, for the issues of this war will be decided not on the ocean, not in the air, not upon the field of battle—it will be decided in the hearts of the men and women of Bristol.'

But another discreet local survey was carried out in shelters, rest centres and evacuation centres by Child Guidance clinic staff, from December 1941, to find out if breaking point was being reached, and to discover the extent of nervous breakdown. According to replies, one-in-four to one-in-six people could not stand up to prolonged anxiety, and in Bristol, there might be 110,000 people in the category of 'suffering from nerves'.

'The proportion of temperamentally unstable people in the population proved to be somewhat higher than had been believed before the war,' concluded this report. A psychiatrist claimed from teachers' reports on 8,000 Bristol children who had been evacuated that there were about eight times as many cases of psychological disturbance amongst those who remained in the city each night as amongst those who had gone to the tunnels on the outskirts.

Poor health affected morale, too: the Medical Officer of Health for Bristol found that air-raids affected hygiene. 'The usual bedtime bath was forgotten on most occasions and the significance of this was not apparent until children were examined for evacuation.' Approximately 15 per cent (3-20 per cent of the population, according to locality) were found to be infested with head lice.

There was a big increase in scabies and impetigo, due to shelter life and changed habits in the home: from 200 cases per year before the war, the number of cases rose to 9,000 in 1942.

'There was an epidemic of impetigo in the Portway shelter—not surprisingly because we never took our clothes off. We went to Tower Hill for treatment and then to the baths in Broadweir, where we were rubbed with ointment after a hot bath.'

Memories like this come back after prompting, but distance generally lends enchantment to the view. Over the years, people tend to gloss over the less admirable aspects of blitz life, and a myth grows up about the way things were.

But which is the true picture of Bristol morale? From an objective viewpoint, nearly 50 years later, expert commentators on the Home Front, like Tom Harrisson, tend to the view that the Mass Observation report on Bristol's low morale was in essence correct.

As he said in his book *Living Through The Blitz:* 'There has been a massive, largely unconscious cover-up of the more disagreeable facts of 1940-41 . . . Memory has transformed events . . . The only valid information for this sort of social history is that recorded at the time, on the spot.'

A Christmas party in the crypt of St. Paul's, Southville, for 130 children whose homes had been damaged by bombs.

Passed, because the message was a happy one: All children safe at Homeopathic. The newspapers would not have been allowed to name the hospital.

Above: Passed. Homeless families getting a meal at a rest centre, after being bombed out of their homes.

Left: Unlike the Stoke Gifford couple, these ladies were happy enough to satisfy the censor. 'Mrs Rothwell, left, was washing up at the time a bomb fell on her home. She was blown the length of the passage but escaped injury.' She lived at Avonmouth.

A chef from Jones's department store carries on regardless, cooking in the ruins of Mary-le-Port Street.

Above: Officials visit the devastated Palmyra Street in Bedminster.
Below: Churchill's visit to Bristol on April 12th, 1941.

Not passed. These Bristol evacuees did not look cheerful enough for the censor.

Nurses at the Homeopathic survey the chaos of what was an orderly ward.

Opposite: Not passed, because of the grim expressions of these Dunkirk survivors being kitted out at a Bristol depot.

Passed. Jolly sailors work on the task of clearing Bridge Street.

3 — *The Yellow Convoy*

This was the cruel nickname in Bristol for the people who, during the height of the Blitz, left the city every night for a refuge in the countryside.

Trekking, another name for it, was not just a Bristol phenomenon. When the big raids started, people from Coventry, Plymouth and Southampton, did the same. A Liverpool train that left each evening bearing hundreds of businessmen out of the city was known as the Funk Express.

Bristolians of all classes went trekking. The better-off would rent a room out in the countryside and take the whole family there by car each evening. 'You couldn't get a room anywhere for love nor money,' says Ronald Coles, who worked at Bristol Aeroplane Company as a draughtsman.

'We lived on Bedminster Down and every evening we drove off to Failand to a room we rented. We managed to get the petrol because my father was a builder. Every spare room for miles was let out. When my department was evacuated to Clevedon I managed to get a cottage in Yatton for £1 a week. I was earning £4 a week at the time. A controlled rent would have been about 12s.6d.'

Mr. Coles remembers another exodus, by the so-called Filton Harriers. 'At Bristol Aeroplane works, after the first daylight raid in September, every time the alert went, there was a mass exodus from the factory, on foot and on bikes, off to the nearest open country, as fast as you could go. The workers didn't trust the shelters at the factory, which were only two or three feet under the surface, so hundreds of us took to our heels and fled out of the nearest works gate.

'We went to Filton golf course, or to a railway tunnel with alcoves in the wall where you could shelter when the trains went through: we felt anywhere was safer than the works. The Company did try to stop it, they locked the gates, but the workers just burst through them. It wasn't an organised flight, it was spontaneous, and probably about a thousand of us did it.' The Filton Harriers only finally gave up their 'run' as the raids diminished.

To those who wanted to spend the night out of Bristol, farmers let rooms, as did publicans and post-mistresses. 'I went on the train every day, after school, on the Frome line, from Brislington to Clutton, to stay with the post-mistress, and I went back again early in the morning. I was only ten, and it made a very long day for me.'

But petrol was rationed, and car ownership was not so common. The poorer families either clubbed together to run a car, or got lifts on lorries, at 1s each. The lorries would stop in a country lay-by and the occupants would sleep the night there, in the back of the lorry. Sometimes the passengers were left to sleep in the hedgerows and fields.

Some areas organised coaches to go out nightly to a village where the village hall was used for sleeping, a custom which caused an upset among the local people. A complaint came to the Town Clerk from a resident of Felton about Bristol people who had come at night and gained access to the village hall without authority. The Clerk to Thornbury R.D.C. complained of the conditions caused by unofficial Bristol evacuees occupying a disused schoolroom, where adults slept at night.

Those who obeyed the Ministry advice to 'Stay Put' were also angry about the trekkers.

'People going out to the countryside were a sore point. They left others to do the firewatching and their attitude was "let their blasted houses burn" ' says a former Bristol docker who, with his mates, used to recite jeering verses and boo at the hundreds of people who had left their homes to shelter in the Portway Tunnel. 'There was a lot of ill-feeling; we didn't agree with it, leaving their homes unwatched. People should have looked after their own property.

'We can tell you of the ones with cars who made their way each night to the safety of the countryside and left it to us to fight fires in the streets where they lived. We were really angry with them.'

People would travel as far as 30 miles out of the city, and the put-upon villagers began to feel the strain. In December 1940, Lady Clare Smyth-Piggot suggested that 'more accommodation should be made available in the area of Brockley Coombe for the convenience of persons from Bristol who are making a practice of spending the night there.'

Brockley and Burrington Coombes were popular refuges because of the protection offered by the rocks and caves: V.A. Maund, the Bristol housewife who kept a wartime diary, noted on December 8th, 1940: 'Out in the car in afternoon, tea at the Bungalow Cafe, Burrington Coombe. We saw a large colony of caravans occupied by people who have fled from the city, parked off the Rock of Ages, and the cafe proprietor told us that cottagers and farmers are besieged by people wanting night accommodation.

'Many sleep in their cars along the Coombe and at the side of the road, with tarpaulins and tents. Washing hangs on lines tied to the rocks, and cooking pots and children are scattered around—the colony has grown, and the gorge reminds me of a refugee camp.'

A country clergyman in the Brockley Coombe area reported that during December to January, 1940-41, up to 1,000 strangers had asked for assistance. Some had even come in pyjamas. He had room in his church house for 50. Country people complained that they were disturbed at night by wandering strangers, who knocked at the doors in the hope of finding lodgings.

It is hard to judge how widespread trekking from Bristol was; contemporary commentators compared the nightly exodus to Piccadilly in the rush hour, or a Bank Holiday crowd. A Bristol clergyman with 953 houses in his parish said that 121 were compulsorily evacuated, 80 were voluntarily evacuated, and 235 were left empty at night. In some areas of the city, between 4 per cent and 10 per cent of the population moved out of the city or went out each night.

The Corporation found that even some of its own officers were illegally using their supplementary petrol allowances to trek out into the country.

Another idea was to go out to village pubs at Dundry and Chew Magna, and spend the evening there. If the siren went, they stayed overnight; if it did not, they returned back to Bristol. This became the fashion with young single people, who were scornfully called the Yellow Convoy by those who stayed at home to do the fire-watching and fire-fighting.

The authorities were very worried by the trekkers, mainly because their homes were left empty at night, easy prey to incendiary bombs which, if not put out, would start fires which could spread to neighbouring property.

So various threats were made, that the ARP wardens would be given the right to break into empty houses, or that homeless families would be billeted there in the owner's absence.

Another fear was of a mass evacuation into the surrounding countryside: the panic and chaos caused in 1940, when France was invaded, and thousands of refugees left their homes to clog the roads was something the British were determined to prevent.

'Stay Put' campaigns were launched, and the vast majority of Bristolians did just that: but it is estimated that at the height of the Blitz, some ten thousand left the city every night.

Sir Hugh Elles, the Regional Commissioner told his superiors at the Ministry of Home Security in a report written early in 1941 that the tendency to 'scuttle' would only be cured by the moulding of public opinion, 'and I suggest very strongly that public opinion must be led by a ministerial pronouncement.' Sir Hugh said that these 'weaknesses' were nasty and dangerous exceptions to Bristol's firm home-front morale.

But Staying Put meant using the despised and inadequate Bristol shelters, a subject which inflamed the entire local population. It was the one issue which brought the people into open rebellion against the authorities, and it led to a scandal: the notorious case of the Portway Tunnel Shelter still looms large in some minds to this day.

A rare picture of a shelter party, in this case in Bedminster, Christmas 1940.

A trench shelter in College Green, 1939. The child in the foreground is picking crocuses.

Above: Rehearsals for war: Soldiers practise marching in gas masks, on the Downs in 1939.

Below: Bristol's Regional War Cabinet in session in their secret War Room, in the cellars of Woodland Road, Bristol.

Left to right: H.M. Webb, City Engineer and A.R.P. Controller, George Gibbs, his second-in-command, General Sir Hugh Elles, Regional Controller, his military advisor, and Alderman Frank Parish, Committee Chairman.

Passed. 'A.R.P. Workers Stick To Their Posts. These women A.R.P. workers were in this cellar when a bomb exploded outside. They calmly carried on with their work during an air raid attack on the South-West.'

The entrance to the Portway Tunnel shelter where as many as 3,000 people turned up to fight for a place inside.

4 — *'It's just like our Council'*

When war was declared, Bristol was in a pathetic state of unreadiness. The city had just 3,500 shelter places ready, though the Home Office calculated that places for 25,000 people were needed. Only 50 of the 200 ambulances needed were available—at one critical stage, ambulance staff at Easton were told to collect the dead in dust carts. They refused to do so.

Moreover, the shelters that had been built were mainly surface structures, brick-built rectangles with thick concrete roofs. No-one trusted them, quite rightly as it turned out, for an error had been made by the Ministry of Home Security in the formula for mixing the mortar. If a bomb had fallen on one of these shelters, the bricks would have collapsed, and the occupants would have been crushed by the concrete slab on top. The one in Dowry Parade, Hotwells, collapsed even before it could be used, and the supporting arch gave way in a shelter in Bedminster.

These defective shelters were duly dismantled (they fell like a pack of cards) and new ones built, but by then no-one had any faith in them. Because these shelters were despised, they were vandalised, used as urinals and refuse tips, and covered in graffiti—'We want bomb-proof shelters' was a common one. In May 1940, the Emergency Committee was told that damage to shelters at Wedmore Vale, Melvin Square, Bedminster Down and Eastville was so bad that they would be ineffective and probably dangerous in an air raid.

Mass Observers in Bristol collected comments on the shelter provision: 'It's wicked, having the worst raids in the country and having no proper underground shelters.' 'There's no excuse for not having proper shelters.' 'It's a waste of money to go on building those doll-houses' (brick shelters). 'Deep shelters have got to come before the end of the war. It's going to drive people scatty unless they have them.' 'We won't win the war unless we have underground shelters for everyone.' 'It's buggery in them' (surface shelters).

MO also visited shelters and reported that many of the trench type were unusable because they were under two feet of water. 'It's a waste of time to build them, nobody uses them,' and 'It's just like our Council. They always realise their mistakes about ten years too late', were comments overheard.

After the first serious raid on Bristol, there was an outcry about the shelters, and a demand that tunnels should be dug into Bristol's seven hills. Petitions were sent to the City Council and the Lord Mayor, and letters were written to the Royal family.

The Regional Commissioner and the civil authorities dismissed this clamour for tunnel shelters as the work of communist agitators, but in fact all sections of the population were begging for them; the Chamber of Commerce sent a letter pleading for deep shelters, and some Bristolians said they were ready to stop war work altogether while the energies of the city were devoted to tunnelling shelters.

Thus began a Bristol obsession with tunnels, ending in open rebellion.

Bristolians came to believe that tunnels were the only safe form of shelter, and began to take refuge, both officially and very unofficially, in a strange assortment of caves, tunnels, mines and railway cuttings.

These included, according to Bristolians who answered an appeal for details, a mine-shaft tunnel in Knapps Lane, St. George, 'an old coal pit tunnel 150 yards long, with thousands of tons of slag piled on top. We children were sent there with a bottle of water and a slice of bread. It was full of water and very unhealthy; I blame my arthritis on this tunnel. A whole family who had TB sheltered there.' (Bristol was famous before the war for its high incidence of Tuberculosis).

The disused Clifton Rocks Railway was another strange shelter. The BBC had taken over part of it, as had BOAC, but the top end was adapted for a public shelter, with each family perched on a series of concrete steps: 'It was very wet and smelly, you had to sit away from the walls to keep dry.' 'We had concerts and fancy dress parties there, it was a real social centre.'

Redcliffe caves were another refuge, but hardly a safe one. 'Very dreary, we squatted where we could. The Vicar used to come to say prayers.' When bombs demolished Redcliffe Infants' School, a crater actually penetrated right down to the cavern below.

Railway tunnels where trains were still running were another risky form of shelter: Ashley Down tunnel was used, as was the railway tunnel that runs by the Portway under Sea Walls. 'We sheltered in a hole in the river bank, and when the alert went, we ran into the tunnel. If a train came, we stood in the alcoves with our faces to the wall, so the train drivers wouldn't see and report us.'

The tunnel under the railway at the end of Mina Road was also fully used. 'People brought mattresses and sofas, there must have been 150 of us on the pavement each side. We couldn't use the road, traffic was still going through. It was better than a surface shelter: the one in Mina Road park was demolished by a bomb and all inside were killed.'

A small cave up in the rock ten feet above Bridge Valley Road held 12 people: 'There was a special knock to get in', and the cave below the end of Windsor Terrace was a shelter too, though luckily it was not until after the war that some of the roof fell in.

The old ice house behind Colston Boys' School, on the banks of the River Frome at Stapleton was another choice; and, perhaps strangest of all, a few sheltered beside the Frome, where it runs underground beneath the heart of the city. 'My uncle was Keeper of the Frome, and he took family and a few neighbours down some steps to the towpath by the river, under the city streets.'

Blaise Mansion's cellars were an official shelter and so was a tunnel that leads from the house to Blaise Hamlet; crowds went to another long tunnel below Willsbridge Hill. 'Damp and smelly, we spent whole nights there, 6pm to 6am, for months.'

The bonded warehouses in Clift House Road were also used, and so was a tunnel in Queen's Avenue, next to the old Embassy cinema; the crypts of churches were popular, though risky; when fire broke out in St. Michael's Church, the 300 people in the crypt below had to flee for their lives, and a number sheltering in the crypt of St. Barnabas lost their lives when the church was bombed.

The civil authorities were very worried by this passion for unorthodox deep shelters, and to do them justice, they had good reason. They had no evidence that these caves and tunnels would withstand a direct hit, and the City Engineer feared that hundreds of tons of rock or brick falling onto a big crowd would cause terrible casualties. They discouraged people from sheltering in large numbers because the potential death toll would be so great.

But Bristolians were obstinate: they said they only felt safe when 'buried in rock'. Attempts to shift them from these refuges were ineffective, and nowhere more so than in the Portway tunnel, scene of the worst public confrontation of the whole Bristol Blitz. It was here that a veritable battle broke out among the civil authorities, the Regional Commissioner and the people. It ended with a sit-in, a visit from the police, a sacking, and telegrams to Buckingham Palace.

When the war started in earnest, people remembered the tunnels that had been built in the rock of the Avon Gorge for the defunct Port and Pier Railway. These had been sealed off when the Portway was built.

There was one long disused stretch, 525 feet long, running under Bridge Valley Road, and a local committee was formed to petition for its opening and conversion into a shelter.

Agitation began as early as May 1940, and a leading campaigner to get the tunnel opened was Mr. St. John Reade, a schoolmaster at Clifton College. He was appointed a Shelter Marshal for the district, and got together a committee of local people to prepare the tunnel for occupation. The first shelterers took possession in November 1940.

They had failed to persuade the Corporation to make any improvements, and conditions were atrocious.

A Mass Observer visited Portway shelter in December 1940. 'There is no sign, but two printed paper notices with an arrow pointing in. Just inside there is a blast wall of sandbags. As one enters, the stench is overpowering, a mixture of sandbags, urine, disinfectant, sweat and bedding. For about the first 50 yards one has to walk through water two inches deep, over bumps in the ground. On each side, beds are standing in water. Sometimes blankets or an old mack is placed on the mud. This water is spring water and comes from a spring where people fill their kettles. It is a simple business to divert this water out but Bristol Corporation has refused them permission.

Consequently all night long, water is pouring into the shelter like a miniature waterfall. Father along it is drier, and there is the great congestion. About half a dozen families have tent arrangements of sackcloth thereby ensuring a certain stuffy privacy.

'A little over half way along there is another brick wall. Beyond this the walls are whitewashed and bunks four across have been built. The poorest and dirtiest people of them all are using this end. The children are four to a bunk. Lighting is by candles and oil lamps. Some distance from the other end is a brick wall with sackcloth; on the other side are closets labelled M and W. The closets are never empty for more than 30 seconds at a time; they have to serve 1,000 people. There is a stinking tang of chlorine. Beyond is the open air.'

On another visit, the observer noted: 'I saw nine cars outside, one of them a 27hp Darracq. The people start coming in at 1pm and before blackout there is only room for half the people to sit down.'

Lord Horder, who was head of a committee set up to investigate conditions in shelters, said of the Portway tunnel that it 'deserved full marks for having everything that a shelter should not possess.'

Yet this was the mecca to which increasing hordes of people came night after night: as word got round that this was the safest shelter in the west, as many as 3,000 would literally fight for a place inside, and they came from as far away as Knowle and Filton. It was said that even some bombed-out people from Coventry came there, too. All classes used the shelter: 'People from posh Clifton houses used to turn up and those who looked drab and grubby got in.'

'It was like a stream of refugees arriving: if you didn't get there by 4.30pm to stake your place, you were too late. There was a lot of jealousy about getting a place.' 'I used to think as a child that the shelter people looked like cave-men, sitting there in the dark and the stink.'

Yet a vital social life sprang up, with parties, contests, entertainments, hymn-singing and games. 'Everyone lost their inhibitions, and the most stuck-up often were the most entertaining.'

But in the official view, there was only room for 200 people, and the Corporation was forced to act. The reasons for their delay were very suspect. For a start, the Corporation had bomb-proofed other tunnel space on the Portway for storing Civic treasures and archives, items from the City Museum and Art Gallery, and Corporation records. This in itself caused anger: people felt their lives were considered less important than costly objects.

But there was a deeper and more secret reason which explained the Corporation's reluctance to allow the Portway Tunnel to be used as a shelter. Bristol "war cabinet" plans against invasion included the use of the tunnel as an emergency broadcasting station, where the BBC would issue emergency bulletins and instructions to the entire South-west region. This was the real reason for keeping the shelterers out.

The one respectable reason the Corporation had for objecting to the tunnel's use was that the City Engineer believed it to be unsafe, and the Medical Officer thought it was insanitary and a danger to health. Once again the authorities concluded that communists were at the root of a campaign to discredit surface shelters.

The whole affair went right to Cabinet level. In January 1941, the Regional Commissioner, Sir Hugh Elles, wrote to explain the situation to Herbert Morrison: 'Upwards of 1,500 persons had formed a sort of gipsy encampment in this indescribable place and filled it with beds, little shelters and a widespread collection of junk of all sorts,' he wrote. 'It is probable that we may have to take drastic measures and be drawn to forcible eviction.'

From the end of November, the Corporation was planning to evict all but 200 people, who would be given tickets to gain entrance, but the deadline was endlessly extended because of the outcry this caused, and also because the police said they would not use force if the shelter marshals failed to persuade people to leave. All through December and January, repeated attempts were made to get people to leave, but after the heavy air-raids of January 3rd, even more people turned up, and the authorities feared a mutiny if an eviction was attempted.

Meanwhile the BBC was ready to move in, and on January 1st they lined up wagons full of equipment on the Portway. The 800 occupants staged a sit-in: the women and children stayed in the tunnel all day, instead of going home as they usually did; the police arrived, decided against forcible eviction, and BBC wagons had to leave.

The occupants of the tunnel got organised: telegrams were sent to Morrison and to the King and Queen, and deputations went to the Corporation; in the Public Record Office there are several pathetic letters to the Queen from shelter users, saying that they were 'suffering from nerves' and would not feel safe in the shelters offered as alternatives at Blaise Mansion cellars and the Clifton Rocks Railway. 'These places do not give the sense of complete burial.' Many sufferers from nerves persuaded their doctors to sign certificates saying they needed to be allowed to stay in the tunnel.

At last the Corporation agreed to carry out a proper conversion of the tunnel, to make it more waterproof and install bunks, and to provide proper sanitation and ventilation. But this would be done if the number of official shelterers could be restricted to 200.

It was only thanks to the persuasive powers of St. John Reade and the shelter committee that eventually, on January 24th, the excess population moved out peacefully, limiting the occupants to 200. Sir Hugh Elles wrote a rather cynical note to Herbert Morrison: 'The redundant population together with their goods and chattels has been winkled out. A few tears but no real trouble. The matter has been very skilfully conducted.'

A casualty of this operation was St. John Reade, who was ignominously sacked from his post of Shelter Marshal. He did not take his dismissal lying down, but continued to turn up for duty. He wrote several angry letters to the Emergency Committee, and had the support of the Revd. Mervyn Stockwood in his battle for re-instatement.

By April 14th, all the official 200 shelterers were moved out, in order to clean the tunnel thoroughly and carry out conversion and improvements, costing £4,257. Typically there was even a row about this for expenditure of only £3,703 was approved. Elles sent a telegram to Morrison: 'All Portway users to clear out. Invalid and nerve cases with no means of transport elsewhere offered alternative accommodation eight-and-a-half and two miles away. The remaining malcontents can accommodate themselves where they can'.

It was one of the most ignoble episodes of the Bristol Blitz, and the memory still rankles. Even now, however, some people remember that dismal tunnel with affection. One man who sheltered there as a child says: 'That place ought to have a plaque on it. It saved hundreds of lives.'

The attached submission No. 107350 may be published (as censored) if, and when its contents satisfy the conditions laid down in the Private and Confidential Letter to Editors re Air Raid Damage of 5.12.40.

Senior Press Censor,
Home News.

Date

PRESS & CENSORSHIP BUREAU

31 DEC 1940

PASSED AS CENSORED

29

Newspaper editors had to deal with endless Ministry of Information bureaucracy before being allowed to publish photographs.

Opposite: Wine Street the morning after the November 24th raid.

Bristol can take it. The Provident Clothing & Supply Co. announced their removal to Gloucester Road from St. James' Barton and donated the price of a Spitfire in response.

Opposite: Passed. 'These people are standing in the crater caused by a bomb which exploded near a Bristol church. Although there were 400 sheltering in the crypt, no-one was injured.' St. Michael's, St. Michael's Hill.

Passed. 'Pathetic glimpse of the raid on Bristol. Sons and neighbours clearing the debris in search of their mother, who was buried beneath the ruins.' Bedminster.

Opposite: Passed. 'Rescue workers burrowed through the wreckage of a house which received a direct hit during a raid on a West town to rescue alive a man and a woman trapped for several hours.'

One of the most famous of the Bristol Blitz pictures: a frozen fire-ladder, useless in the freeze-up of winter 1941. W.V.S. workers recall that even hot tea froze in the cup.

Opposite: Sight-seers in Park Street assess the damage the day after the November 24th raid.

DEMBO

The first bomb of the Bristol Blitz fell here in Lower Maudlin Street, June 25th, 1940.

Castle Street, November 25th, 1940.

Not passed. A Bristol bus trapped in the wreckage of a bombed warehouse in Prince Street.

All that remained of the busy Bridge Street, after clearing up and demolition, November 1940.

GLW 424
HOME BREWED

Graphic illustration of what the fire-fighters were up against, as fire rages in Pritchard Street near Newfoundland Street. Note the dozens of spectators.

Another famous photograph of the Bristol Blitz, capturing the mournful shattered roofline of Union Street, looking upwards from the Odeon.